The 5am

Playbook

The Complete Strategy to
start an early rising habit
(so you can find the time
to live your dreams)

BRYCE CHAPMAN

The 5am Playbook
The Complete Strategy to start an early rising habit (so you can find the time to live your dreams)

By

Bryce Chapman

ISBN-13: 978-1518729263

ISBN-10: 1518729266

Published and Distributed by

**Bryce Chapman and
5am Wake Up Call
P.O. Box 900
Narrabeen, NSW, 2101, Australia**

admin@5amwakeupcall.com

www.5amwakeupcall.com

*** WARNING ***

FOLLOWING THE STRATEGY OUTLINED IN THIS BOOK MAY RESULT IN HAPPINESS, IMPROVED HEALTH AND FITNESS, WEALTH, FUN, WEIGHT LOSS, IMPROVED DISCIPLINE, CHASING A DREAM, SUPER-PRODUCTIVITY, GETTING AHEAD OF THE DAY, FINDING YOUR PASSION, RESPECT, WORK PROMOTION, GETTING OUT OF YOUR COMFORT ZONE, STARTING BUSINESSES, A UNIVERSITY DEGREE, WRITING A BOOK, LEARNING THE GUITAR, FOCUS, DOING 50 PULL-UPS, LEAVING THE RAT RACE, HAVING A DREAM JOB, SELF CONFIDENCE, BECOMING A LEADER, FINDING YOUR MAGNIFICENT OBSESSION, BEING FASCINATING, LEARNING A NEW LANGUAGE, SEEING THE SUN RISE, REDUCED BUSY-NESS, INCREASED LEVELS OF SATISFACTION, TIME WITH YOUR KIDS, BURNING BRIDGES, AVOIDING HANGOVERS, BEATING DEADLINES, AVOIDING TRAFFIC, REDUCING STRESS, YOGA, GOING TO BED EARLIER, READING, WALKING THE DOG, GOAL SETTING, A DIPLOMA, INVENTING SOMETHING, ADVENTURES, HOT AIR BALLOONING, THROWING OUT THE FAT CLOTHES, PLAY, IMPRESSING THE BOSS, BECOMING RELIABLE, SUCCESS, REMOVAL OF LIMITS, BEING POSITIVE, INDEPENDENCE, SELF-IMPROVEMENT, DOING 100 PUSH-UPS, PUTTING YOU FIRST, BRAIN ACTIVITY AND NEUROPLASTICITY, ACTION, IMPROVED DECISION MAKING, A GOOD REPUTATION, JOGGING, PLANNING, DILIGENCE, EATING A HEALTHY BREAKFAST, LIST MAKING, A NEW MINDSET, CHALLENGING YOURSELF, TIME FOR FRIENDS, BECOMING AN ENTREPRENEUR, BUYING A BEACH HOUSE, LIVING LONGER, LIVING A BIGGER LIFE, CATCHING THE EARLY WORM, WAKING UP KNOWING YOU ARE LIVING A NEW (AND IMPROVED) RICH LIFE, AND MANY OTHER CHANGES WHICH MAY BE IRREVERSIBLE.

PLEASE CONSULT YOUR INNER-SELF BEFORE UNDERTAKING THIS STRATEGY.

"I was sceptical when Bryce told me that getting up at 5am would make me happier and more Productive (and let me sleep more). But he was so passionate about it, I had to listen. Then I started reading about the science of a 5am life. I looked at the success stories. And (most important) I tried it! Establishing my 5am habit was a lot easier than I thought it would be (I've never been a morning person; in fact, I almost flunked out of college because of it). Now I'm more focused and productive. I'm working out again for the first time in 20 years. My business is booming. I have more confidence. And I'm having more fun. That's because success is fun (so is feeling like you're in control of your life)! Even my marriage is better (it wasn't bad before... but if you're an entrepreneur or work in the corporate world you know the strain that all those hours can put on your relationships).

If you're thinking about becoming a 5amer, or if you want to take your existing 5am life to the next level, check out Bryce's website and set up an introductory call with him. Bryce is the real deal."

Mark Malatesta

Founder of Literary Agent Undercover and former
NY Times bestselling literary agent

Boulder, Colorado, USA

***

"Thanks to Bryce I've been getting up at 5am nearly every day for three months.

It's one of the most powerful tools I have to transform my life, and the lives of those I love."

Peter Cerneaz.

Artist and business owner.

Bellevue Hill, NSW, Australia

***

Bryce Chapman's 5am Wake Up Call is so much more than the early bird catches the worm, it is a call to arms. He helps you 'take action' to being what, where, who you want to be; to live your dreams. Stop living an accidental life, letting others dilute your precious time, sapping your energy. Pinpoint exactly what you want and aim for it! Whether writing a book, music, film script, creating a business, increasing sales, selling a business, getting fit, learning a language, to dance, studying for a degree, acquiring promotion. Whatever your dream Bryce's 5 Am lifestyle choice will help you get it, using fact not faith. It is so simple, they should teach it at schools. Bravo Bryce for collating all the information we need into one short course... you are creating a legacy of high achievers, which is what 'man' should be. Thank you.

Siobhan C Cunningham

Author/Screenwriter

London, UK

Table of Contents

Table of Contents continued...

The Game

The last ten years has been an incredible ride that has seen my life improve in more ways than I could have ever imagined, and it all started with a single impulse.

Back in 2005, at the age of 39, I started an experiment of waking up at 5am every weekday morning so that I could focus on my own life, which I knew, must be improved.

If you could have spent a few days with me back then, you would have see how busy I was, running hard on the treadmill of life, day after day, week after week. You would have also seen that when I did find a chance to stop and take a breath, I was unsatisfied with the direction of my life, and that I had a fearful feeling that I was living an accidental life, unplanned and uncontrolled. To be fair, I had actually been successful in business, but the business wasn't my dream and I had never planned on being in it for so long, trapped in the dangerous place of working head down without fully knowing where I was going, and what it was actually costing me. Month after month, year after year, on and on, I pushed forward! You may have even thought that I had made it when I could finally take time off regularly. But the reality was, I could never really switch off and the pressure was never actually released. My life was controlled by my business and this had been going on for over 18 years!

I was also an active father of four and loving husband struggling to get the work – life balance thing happening. Under the circumstances, you would have thought I did a pretty good job, but the pressure was starting to build up; I was feeling burnt out, too busy, frustrated, angry, vulnerable, and overwhelmed.

I was heading for a train wreck.

"How had this all happened and what happened to all my dreams?"

The truth is my dreams had been de-prioritized as I built the business and became a father, in an attempt to build the foundations for a good life. The problem was that I hadn't given enough priority to the dreams I once had and that loss started to play on my mind. I didn't go down without a fight however, and energized by creative seizures I would work passionately on a project, hoping that my dream might finally work out. But they would always fail. The foundations of the life I had created were too weak!

Busy, busy, busy! Day after day, after day!

The incredible relationship I had with my second wife was now starting to show major signs that things were under strain: busy life, failed dreams, pressure, and the feeling of being overwhelmed.

I was now at breaking point!

That was when I had the impulse to wake up early to find the time to make a change!

It started slowly, just a couple a mornings a week to go for a walk on the beach and listen to Tony Robins with my CD Walkman.

Then the urge to start running (having never been a jogger) came over me with such power and focus, which saw my routine step up a level and my energy level rise even more. I felt great!

I then started to go to work at 5:30 am so I could get on top of my day (ahead of the distractions) and leave on time and without stress. This gave me the time to enjoy my family, exercise, and life.

It worked; I couldn't believe it! I found that the focus at that time of the day was intense, as I had no distractions. What I did in two hours would have taken me four or five (if not all day) if I had started normally.

I had discovered super-productivity!

Now that business was under control, I started to plan my future by mind mapping my entire life to reveal all my options and take massive action to make it the best life possible. My new Rich Life.

The results were incredible and within two years, I had positioned and successfully sold my primary business (the one that took up 90% of my time), allowing me to redirect my energy. I now earned way more by doing much less with one of the other business activities, which had up until then, been totally under-utilized.

This gave me the time and freedom to work on my dreams (my Magnificent Obsession) to be a creator by writing and coaching whilst still being a loving husband, enthusiastic father, and in control of the other essential foundations to my New Rich Life being: 1. Health & Fitness; 2. Family & Friends; 3. Happiness; 4. Wealth; and 5. Work (but more about those later).

I had taken control of my life!

So why do you want to wake up at 5am? What dreams are you going to chase?

Do you want to become that fit person of your dreams or lose that 30lbs.? Perhaps you want to write a book, start a business, or re-train by getting a degree? Maybe you just want to get on top of a busy life so you can return home early and spend time with your kids?

Whatever the reason, I know many of you have tried waking up early before, but have failed. Others may have thought about it but never had the courage to take on the challenge with conviction. Still others may have just had the impulse for the first time, that maybe something great can come from an early morning habit.

Well, as founder of 5am Wake Up Call I have tried and tested most ways to get out of bed early, so I am more than qualified to now share my complete playbook. Over ten years of trial and error has resulted in this playbook and there is simply no other guide available anywhere in the world that reveals such a complete strategy for succeeding at waking up early; believe me, I have looked! I have literally thrown myself into a decade long experiment to see if this habit can be long lasting, enjoyable, and more importantly, can make a real difference to my life.

It will be up to you to decide which Plays are right for you and to take them on with discipline, persistence, and focus. But, you will discover that it is possible to wake up at 5am, it can be enjoyable and it will change your life forever! I would also predict that it will change your life much more than you ever thought possible.

After all, the list of Famous 5amers is long and strong:

- Peter the Great (Emperor of Russia);
- Christopher Columbus (explorer);
- Benjamin Franklin (founding father of the U.S.A.);
- Thomas Jefferson (founding father of the U.S.A);
- George Washington (1st President U.S.A.);
- Daniel Webster (U.S Senator);
- Ernest Hemingway (author);
- Toni Morrison (author);
- John Grisham (author);
- Gwyneth Paltrow (actress);

- Ian Thorpe (Olympic swimmer);
- Tiger Woods (golf);
- Sugar Ray Leonard (boxing);
- Muhammad Ali (boxing);
- Padmasre Warrior (business);
- William Cook (business);
- Howard Schultz (Starbucks);
- Donald Trump (business/politics);
- Ingvar Kamrad (IKEA);
- Sam Walton (Wal-Mart);
- Warren Buffet (investor);
- George W. Bush (43rd President U.S.A.);
- Barak Obama (44th President U.S.A.);
- Michelle Obama (First Lady);
- Michael Bloomberg (business);
- Rupert Murdock (media).

If you commit to the following strategy outlined in this playbook, you will succeed! If you choose to use that time to focus with discipline and persistence, you will succeed at anything you desire.

Understand that our relationship with bed is paradoxical. We are reluctant to go to bed at night and reluctant to get out of it in the morning. However, in the greater scheme of things, an early rising habit is not asking that much of ourselves. It is only asking that you commit to a relatively minor change to your daily routine and equally important, is not requiring you to go with less sleep.

However, even with the knowledge that by using this strategy you can be working toward those all important dreams and burning desires by bringing your Magnificent Obsession to life, this new habit can be difficult.

Now that you are clear of the challenge I am putting to you, this book will help you by giving you all 20 plays, so that you can not only successfully establish a new habit of early rising, but can also energize your day, increase productivity and give yourself the best chance of achieving your goals.

Or as I like to say, live a New Rich Life.

Let us begin…………

Play #1: Think as an Early Riser

Becoming an early riser all starts with an impulse, that initial thought.

Once you gain discipline with your thoughts, you will also:

1. Remove your self imposed limits;
2. Step out of your comfort zone and into a new life;
3. Set up your entire day for success.

There is only one person who can make the habit of early rising an enjoyable and essential part of your life, a habit you cannot possibly go without, which makes you feel fantastic each waking morning.

That person is you.

No one can force this habit on you. As a young man I was working in British Columbia over one summer, planting pine trees in the wilderness. Thousands of acres of mountainous land had been cleared by logging companies and it all had to be re-planted by hand with new pine tree seedlings. This was extremely hard work, spending each day trekking over the cleared landscape with a backpack full of small trees from sunrise to sunset, 7 days a week. Each morning around 5am the supervisor would walk around the camp playing heavy metal music on a ghetto blaster to wake everyone up. I didn't want to get up. It was dark, very cold, way too early and all I was going to do all day was work very hard at something that at times, I hated. One of the leading contributors to the hardships of that work was the intense moods swings I was subject to, resulting from total exhaustion and the endless task repeated each day. I would go through periods of depression and negativity that would take me very close to breaking point. During those times, I absolutely hated getting up at 5am, but I did anyway, day after day. The heavy metal music would infiltrate my dreams, getting louder and louder until it was outside my Kombi van, waking me up. The realisation that the music was not part of my dreams but a sick and torturous method of being woken up was always shocking. I dragged myself out of bed without fail only because of my determination to finish the season, however, there wasn't a snowball's chance in hell that waking up at 5am was going to become an essential habit; not then anyway. When it was forced on me like that, without the burning desire to get up because it was something that I wanted to do, it was never going to become a habit. When my 'tour' was over, I was back to waking up later from day one.

Being forced to wake up early will not make it develop into a habit unless you first develop the habit in your mind.

When Napoleon Hill coined the phrase and title of his book, *Think and Grow Rich*, he could not have put it any better. You have to use the power of your mind to make early rising something you really want to do.

You literally have to "think and wake up early". At that waking moment, you have to take control of your mind and think with clarity.

You must want to be an early riser.

All the other strategies in this playbook are subservient to this overriding and all-powerful fact, so you will need to work on developing them with clear intent and purposeful thought.

"You have absolute control over but one thing, and that is your thoughts. This is the most significant and inspiring of all facts known to man! It reflects man's divine nature. This divine prerogative is the sole means by which you may control your own destiny. If you fail to control your own mind, you may be sure you will control nothing else."

–Napoleon Hill

Play #2: Have an Extraordinary Reason!

Discovering your major purpose is one of life's greatest quests.

Living a dream is your path to:

1. Being happier, satisfied and healthier;
2. Wealth, riches and fame;
3. Defining your own personal success and achieving it.

The most important device you have for early rising is to give yourself an extraordinary reason to do so. You need a compelling reason to get out of the warm bed in the middle of winter when it is still dark and cold outside, and you're tired. Without such a reason, you will simply fail.

A Magnificent Obsession is that extraordinary reason.

Your life will feel incomplete if you fail to achieve your Magnificent Obsession and your burning desire to make this dream a reality is the ultimate leverage to supercharge the play #1 of thinking to wake up early.

Become obsessed about why you are getting up in the morning. The moment the alarm goes off, think about nothing else but the fact that you are just about to work towards your Magnificent Obsession. Think about how great you feel as you progress closer and closer to its reality. Think about how it is changing your life, defining who you are, and demonstrating to the world that you are willing, able, and passionate about taking control of your life.

Discover your Magnificent Obsession.

Think about changing your life forever.
Think about how being rich will improve your life.
Think about losing all the weight you desire.

Think about being fit and healthy so you can live a long, happy life.

Think about getting that promotion.

Think about starting your own business.

Think about de-stressing your life.

Think about graduating with honours.

Think about getting out of the rat race.

Think about writing that book.

Think about whatever you want to do, whatever your dream is, whatever your Magnificent Obsession is.

Become passionate about achieving your Magnificent Obsession. This is the ultimate alarm clock.

Wake up and get on with it!

"The alarm clock would go off at five, and I'd jump in the shower. My office was five minutes away. And I had to be at my desk, at my office, with the first cup of coffee, a legal pad, and write the first word at 5:30am, five days a week."

– John Grisham

Play #3: Set The Rules

Set yourself up for success every morning, not failure.

Deciding what 5am mornings are for you by setting the rules you live your life by will:

1. Exercise discipline;
2. Allow focus by removing distractions (usually unwanted);
3. Improve decision-making.

Here are three friends of mine with three sets of rules for waking up early.

At 5:45am I was riding by bike to the gym at the surf club with my dog Banjo excitedly running beside me when, out of the dark, I came across a figure jogging toward me. As we approached Banjo stopped the jogger for a pat and I then realised it was a good friend of mine, Jill. Now in her mid-60's Jill still jogs regularly and by all measures is fit, healthy, and happy.

During the earlier years of my experimenting with early rising, I had often talked to Jill about her habit of going out jogging or walking in the mornings 2 to 3 days a week. It was a routine that not only kept her fit and healthy, but also kept her feeling happy, organized, and in control of her life. Earlier in her life with her husband and young family, Jill had experienced the loss of good friends and the constant fear of the violence of South Africa before fleeing with little but their lives to Australia. Having a lady of Jill's quiet and eloquent voice talk about how she would sleep with an Uzi under her bed was incomprehensible to me; after all, we didn't even lock the doors at night. It gave me an understanding of how much Jill enjoys those quiet morning runs before the rest of the day gets underway. She uses that time to set up her day and to maintain her health and fitness, as she is fully aware of the value of life and how to make the most of it.

After finishing the first draft of my manuscript for my upcoming book (stay tuned) I emailed an old friend for some advice on editing. Ted had moved to Australia from New Zealand to be a proof-reader and had helped me out previously when I was writing a television series. Well-spoken and intelligent, his attention to detail from proofreading is obvious and as I had previously talked to Ted about the book I was writing and my 5am habit, he included this note in his reply.

"I get up at 5am three days a week to go to the gym, and between 5:30am and 7am other days. It sure is great to get a good start on those early days. - Ted."

Each morning, when I start writing on my computer, it automatically starts all sorts of unknown software including my Skype connection. This would normally go unnoticed however, some mornings not long after I start writing I receive a small note from Skype letting me know that my good friend of mine (Marcel) has just logged on. His computer has also automatically started up its communications with the outside world, which in this case includes me.

It's coming up to 30 years since I jackarooed (that's Australian for being a rancher) with Marcel but now, he is solidly city-based with a wife and family. Marcel worked successfully for many years as one of Australia's leading financial advisers with a large bank however, was one of the first casualties of the Global Financial Crisis. His life quickly changed as he left the corporate world and started up his own financial business at home. With two young boys Marcel and his wife Lisa, are still in the peak of parenting so running a home-based business often has to take second place. The boundaries of work and home become obscure, so Marcel regularly plans an early start to get the jump on the day; especially when deadlines approach or important meetings are coming up. These early mornings have also allowed Marcel the flexibility to be involved with getting the boys ready for school and to regularly get away camping with them. Some mornings, as my computer alerts me that he is online, we send each other a short message of support but we usually simply get on with our early start knowing that we are working hard on our dreams.

These are three ordinary people living ordinary lives however; all have chosen a certain commitment to an early rising habit.

Jill doesn't want to wake up at 5am every week day as 3 mornings gives her what she needs from the habit; she then enjoys sleeping in a bit the other mornings. Similarly, Ted has decided what days an early rising habit allows him to get to the gym, otherwise it is not so essential. Marcel's 5am habit is flexible depending on his weekly schedule, work demands and family commitments.

All these early rising habits have allowed these people to improve their lives. They have all decided what commitment is right for them and worked towards making that a lasting habit.

The aim of your new habit is to set you up for success, not failure. It is not imposing a set of unsustainable conditions on you that will become unrealistic in a normal life. If that was the case every time you failed to meet that hard set of rules you would feel as if you failed and want to give up, developing a negative mindset of not achieving challenges put to you each day.

So, decide what days are right for you and make that the set of rules you wake up by. Understand the commitment it is going to take and be realistic and supportive; it is better to step up and increase your mornings as your habit becomes an essential start to your day than to back down because the habit is not working in your life. Always remind yourself that you are a success and you are developing the mindset of a successful person, morning by morning, day after day.

Decide what 5am morning will work for you.

Finally, when deciding what 5am habit is right for you also consider any short-term benefits you can gain that will enable you to meet any challenge. I was recently reading an article on the American actor Mark Wahlberg, discussing his role in the movie *Contraband*. Actors like Mark often need months to prepare themselves for a role and then they have to immerse themselves during the shoot which places enormous pressure and demands on their time. The article interviewing Mark discusses some of these issues.

"Today, he again looks fighting fit. "I had to train for the movie that I'm shooting right now," he explains. " In order to do it and have it not affect the rest of my day and schedule, I go to bed at 8:30, then I wake up at 4:30, and I'm in the gym at 5:00 until 6:30. Then I get the kids up and take them to school so I can get home and do my work stuff.""

(Film Ink, March 2012 by Karl Rozemeyer)

Your 5am habit may be essential for you to meet a short-term target or may be something you want to take on as a lifestyle choice. Decide what 5am mornings work for you and set the rules.

"I've only had two rules: Do all you can and do it the best you can. It's the only way you ever get that feeling of accomplishing something."

–Colonel Sanders

Play #4: Pleasure and Pain

To follow through, you must harness the power of leveraging pleasure and pain.

When you understand how pleasure and pain works you will:

1.   Accelerate the power of neuroplasticity;
2.   Access super-productivity;
3.   Increase focus.

It is essential that you associate an immediate and massive amount of pleasure when you get up early. I'm not talking about dragging your weary bones out of bed, through a shower, and into the day passively thinking how good it is that you are using your mind to take control of your life. I'm talking about giving yourself such a shock of pleasure that you will bounce out of bed without hesitation. In fact, you may end up jumping out of bed before the alarm goes off!

For you to do this you need to give yourself an enormous amount of pleasure when you get up early, whenever you're thinking about getting up early and when you are talking to others about getting up early.

Am I being clear? Any association you have with early rising must be linked to pleasure.

Now is the time to put the power of your mind and thinking to work.

You need to have a conversation with yourself and you need to win the argument. It is too easy, even when we are doing an extraordinary job, to be modest in one's mind and just go with the flow without any direct and focused conversation within. From now on you need to become your own personal motivational speaker, life coach, and most avid fan by telling yourself how absolutely fantastic you are for working towards your Magnificent Obsession by waking up early. Cheer yourself on, bet on yourself, arouse all the positive feelings about what you are doing and back yourself every morning. Shout out to yourself that you are finally on your way to getting what you have been dreaming about all that time. It is actually happening. How good is that?

Now that you have motivated yourself, take a further moment to fully appreciate those feelings you have about what a good job you are doing. Understand those feelings you have when you are achieving your goals. Recognise those feelings of being successful. Become completely in touch with those feelings from knowing you are finally on your way to making your dreams come true.

Throughout the day exercise this new skill by giving yourself the reassurance that you are doing an amazing thing. Feel the pleasure of what you are achieving and feel the motivation you have in knowing that now it is all possible. Understand how good you feel.

The leverage of pleasure and pain will deliver the power you require.

It may seem I am overstating this point however, it is essential you gain clarity of these feelings because they are the power behind all that you are trying to achieve. Without them an early rising habit will fail. The dopamine released into the synaptic gaps between your neurons are making you feel great, and will make you want more. That is the key to developing a new habit and to making new mind maps. That is how we bring about change.

Now use these new and developing paths of thought as your waking thoughts each early morning. Use those positive feelings about what a wonderful job you are doing to motivate you to roll out of bed without a second thought and make those dreams come true.

On the flip side, you need to give yourself an immediate and massive amount of pain when you don't get up as planned. If you have simply changed your mind at that waking time and decided to sleep in you need to give yourself some pain by having another (and different) conversation with yourself.

How bad do you feel? You missed an opportunity to change your life and achieve your goals. You have let a morning of working on your dreams go to waste. You have missed the quietude of a new day. You have gone back on your word. You have failed yourself. You will never be successful if you cannot even be disciplined enough to work toward something you dream about. After all, getting up early isn't that hard. How lazy you have been! You have sabotaged your own desires. How stupid was it to sleep in?

If you think this is being too hard, wake up and smell the coffee. If you have gone to sleep the night before with the clear intension of waking up early but have simply changed your mind at that waking hour by deciding to sleep instead of working toward your Magnificent Obsession, your very own dreams and desires, you have failed. Fulfilling your dreams is not always easy. Being successful is not always easy. Setting up your life so you can be happier, healthier, or richer takes self-discipline, self-motivation, and a burning desire.

Now understand that you need to keep moving forward, so use that pain to refocus your early rising habit. Take today's failing as an important lesson that adds power and passion to the pleasure you feel from your habit the next morning.

Understand that even though you may be tough on yourself when you fail to get up early, you are equally kind to yourself when you succeed. You must be able to move past any of those days you break your plan with haste, toward the next successful day you wake up early.

"I'm really not a morning person at all, it's just sheer determination. I'm very strict with myself. When I practice six days a week and eat clean food, I feel much better."

– Gwyneth Paltrow

Play #5: Rewards

Become your own biggest fan by rewarding yourself for all your hard work!

Understanding the importance of self-rewarding will benefit you by:

1. Greater neurotransmitters, meaning greater neuroplasticity;
2. Maintaining your motivation
3. Improving goal setting.

As well as the pleasure (see Play #4) you give yourself mentally with an early rising habit, a physical reward will have great benefits as well by reinforcing your good work with another hit of your body's dopamine (neurotransmitter). It is important to make the link between the reward and the action of rising early. Be clear with yourself that you will earn a particular reward if you keep getting up early and then later, when you receive the reward, congratulate yourself again with purpose.

For example, tell yourself out loud after you wake up early, "I can't wait till I have completed an early rising routine for 3 straight months and I receive my new (_fill in the blank_)."

Don't worry, no one will hear you, and it will only take a few seconds. Throughout that 3 month period, go and look for the particular reward, one that is going to get the heart pumping fast.

I did this with a new surfboard by going down to the local board shop and picking up a few from the rack to get a real life feel until, I found a great "Bear" long board that I loved. Over the next 3 months, I thought about how the long board felt when I was in the shop holding it with the salesman, as well as how much fun I was going to have surfing until after the final morning when I went down and bought it. When my new board was tucked under my arm, I yelled, out loud, "Well done, I succeeded in this great new habit and I am changing my life for the better. Good on me!" Then I went for a surf!

Choose whatever reward you want but, don't be afraid of making it great! You may use smaller rewards with a shorter time frame as well as larger rewards over a longer period. Link the rewards to what you achieve with your early rising habit and make it fun by being creative. After all, you really do deserve it. Remember that this is all up to you. Life can be tough and no one is going to be around to cheer you on, so you have to rely on yourself to give yourself a pat on the back when you achieve your goals. Whether it's the first week, month, or year of a successful early rising habit, it is great work and should be rewarded. You have made a decision to get up and change your life by working hard and persistently on your Magnificent

Obsession. That's good, but it's even better knowing that if you just keep going you will get there, your dreams will come true. Until then, reward yourself without guilt or grief from other people. This is your life and now you are in control.

The power of rewards (my family enjoying our new boat)

Sorry, but there has to be a flip side to this as well, but hopefully you won't need to apply it too often. If you fail to carry out your plan of early rising, going without something physical, as well as the pain mentioned in the previous play will drive it home.

You may have to delay a reward, or go without something that day. Yes, that may hurt, especially if it is something you are looking forward to but, I'm sorry, the pain has to be felt immediately. Having done that you will need to refocus on getting the reward with clear thought so the association with achieving your goal remains strong.

"For every disciplined effort, there is a multiple reward."

– Jim Rohn

Play #6: Motivation

Motivation must be maintained to keep your energy and focus, not just re-ignited casually, without purpose.

When the importance of motivation is implemented you will:

1. Reduce down time;
2. Attract what you seek and fast track success;
3. Improve your mindset, happiness and well-being.

It is natural for your motivation to fluctuate as these plays become habit. For some reason or another you may have a flat day or week where you find getting up especially hard. Even after your 5am Wake Up Call habit has become a well-established routine, you will need to maintain your motivation.

The best way to do this is to focus on your major purpose, your Magnificent Obsession. This is what you want to achieve, who you want to become, and why you are waking up so early so, it should spark your passion and motivate you each waking morning.

Also, focus on the other benefits of a 5am Wake Up Call (to help, I have given you three for each play) that apply to you until they become familiar and until you become passionate about them. Throughout the day and before you go to sleep at night, think of those benefits and feel good that you are taking action to change your life for the better.

You will also be pleased at how many of your friends and acquaintances are interested in why you have chosen a 5am habit. On hearing of the time you wake they will be astonished, so here's a great chance to motivate yourself and perhaps help your friends at the same time, by discussing the benefits with them. By openly and passionately committing to this life in full view of your friends you will be more determined to succeed in your habit.

One way I motivated myself when I was on my way to work in the mornings was think about how many others were also up and going. I was surprised at the number of cars already on the road at that hour and decided that if all these people can get up early, then so can I. In reality I was not asking too much of myself. What was even more motivating was that unlike them, I had made the choice to get up at 5am as part of my new 5am strategy. I was passionate about arriving to work early knowing that I had to motivate my staff, be on top of business (and then prepare it for sale). I was working hard towards my Magnificent Obsession however, most of the other people driving to work are not. I then thought of all the people in the world who get up at

5am or earlier; there must be millions. More so, I imagine many of them don't wake up by choice as I do as a 5amer. Wow, I have no reason to complain about my early morning habit. In fact, I'm lucky because I am doing this because I want to, not because I have to!

There are many ways to keep motivated to stay focused (books, CDs, live events such as Tony Robins), however, understand that it is normal for these levels to rise and fall. Don't be too hard on yourself during times when you are down, you will move past that state of mind before you know it.

Tony Robins, the best motivator in the world, and much more.

Finally, think of all the great people from history who have woken up early and made their lives remarkable. I always take comfort in knowing great leaders like Benjamin Franklin, Sam Walton and Muhammad Ali thought that getting up early was an essential part of their lives.

Be proud to be in the same league.

"Of course motivation is not permanent. But then, neither is bathing; but it is something you should do on a regular basis."

– Zig Ziglar

Play #7: Don't Listen to the Adolescent

The discipline of early rising will exercise your ability to be disciplined and achieve anything and everything else you desire.

Being clear about what you want and disciplined to stay the course will benefit your entire life by:

1. Showing others you are prepared to do what it takes;
2. Improving self-esteem;
3. Reducing your fail rate/increasing your success rate.

When starting your new habit, you may choose to gradually wake up earlier by 15 minutes or so each day, or jump right in by going straight to 5am in one hit. Going straight to 5am can be brutal but your body adapts quickly after all, we don't slowly go into daylight savings or when changing time zones while travelling overseas.

Going straight to 5am allows you to experience the advantages of the early start right from the first morning motivating you to meet the challenge again the following day.

Also, if you are having trouble going to sleep early, don't worry. The sudden change from waking early will reduce this because by the end of the day, or after a few days, you will be looking forward to an early sleep like you have never done before, trust me!

Whatever your strategy is, set out your game plan during the day or the night before, and do not change your rules in the morning.

Your subconscious mind is powerful, highly creative, and can lie to you with such conviction, coming up with a dozen compelling reasons to stay in bed in the morning.

This is because as teenagers, we just loved to sleep in. Our young bodies needed the extra sleep to cope with all the growth and hormonal changes but unfortunately, that experience is entrenched deeply with-in all of us. So when your alarm goes off in the cold, dark morning at 5 am, the remaining imprint of that teenager can be rudely awakened. The adolescent may seize control of the moment and lie to your grown-up mind.

"There's no need to get up at this time of day, you need the sleep". "If you are going to be able to work today you need more sleep". "I think you have a sore throat, so you better get more sleep to avoid getting sick, it's for the best". "I will be able to work on my dreams tonight, so it's okay to stay asleep now". "I think I work better at night anyway, so it's better to sleep a bit more". "I am getting too run down with these stupid early mornings; staying in bed is the right

thing to do". And, "I am doing the right thing by staying in bed, I'm still a success."

DON'T LISTEN TO THE ADOLESCENT MIND, IT IS LYING TO YOU!

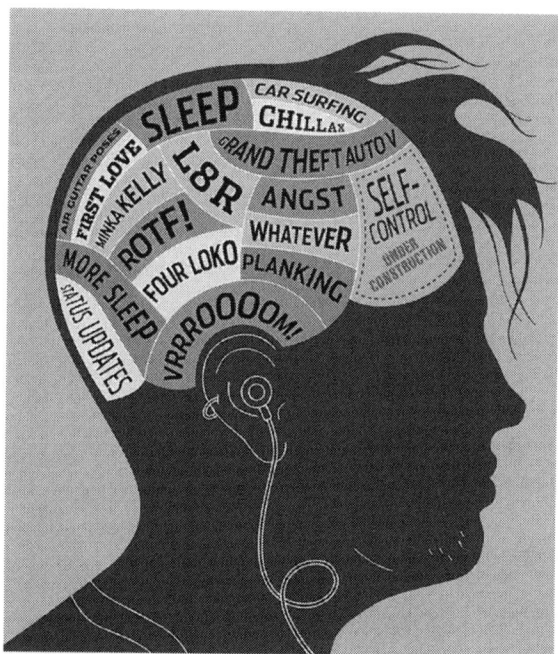

Ignore the adolescent mind.

It is attempting a mutiny and the longer you stay in bed listening to it; the more powerful and likely it will overrun the ship. Get out of bed quickly and start the day, the adolescent teenager will quickly disappear. Then reward yourself with a shot of pleasure. Well done, you are on your way to fulfilling your dreams.

Changing your plans can never be done when you are trying to wake up in the morning. You simply cannot trust yourself, the adolescent may be in control and you will be very disappointed when you finally get up and the adult mind is back in control.

Make any changes the night before when the adolescent is gone and your motivated, adult mind is planning for success.

"Good intentions might sound nice, but it's positive actions that matter."

–Tim Fargo.

Play #8: Early to Bed

This habit is not about getting less sleep, so go to bed earlier if you want to succeed at it!

Going to bed earlier is going to help you:

1. Set your body's clock for a long-term change;
2. Make early rising enjoyable;
3. Prevent burnout.

You cannot expect to make a 5am Wake Up Call habit enjoyable unless you get a good night's sleep. This will mean you have to go to bed earlier.

We need to have at least 7 hours of sleep each night, therefore, you need to be winding yourself down and well organised so at around 9:30pm, you are ready for sleep.

Give up the coffee in the afternoon and evening and try not to drink a lot before going to bed so you don't have to get up in the night to visit the bathroom.

Turn off the TV, stop surfing the Internet or working late, and allow your mind plenty of down time so it is not still in 'go' mode when you try to sleep. Try getting into the habit of reading each night to unwind and get sleepy.

Don't waste your life by staying up late just for the sake of it.

If you share a house with others or are at university, where the trend is to stay up late, you may have a harder job, but don't give up. Go against the trend and impress your friends with your early rising. Demonstrate the results of your new life choice — you may even get them on-board.

Try to go to sleep at the same time each night so your body gets into a good routine. Remember not to worry about not being able to get to sleep early because after you start your routine, it won't be a problem, you will be pleased at how early you want to go to bed.

Becoming a 5amer requires the discipline to get up at that hour in the morning but equally, it requires the discipline of going to bed early the night before. Don't be concerned that you are leaving your friends and family to go to bed. All those concerns will ease as you show by example how you can take on the world and live your dreams with your 5am Wake Up Call.

"Early to bed and early to rise, makes a man healthy, wealthy, and wise."

–Benjamin Franklin

Play #9: Flexibility Trumps Perfection

Perfection is a myth, and when it is a requirement, it will become the reason for quitting.

Having flexibility (within your rules) will:

1. Allow long-term success of your new habit;
2. Let you enjoy all aspects of life;
3. Maintain self-confidence, positive attitude, and motivation.

There may be times when a 5am wake up call is just not possible or sensible. Here's an interesting example. When I had my old business every 8 weeks or so I had to get a new delivery of young lambs that were transported by interstate truck. I would have to meet the truck in the early hours of the morning so, when I returned home it could be 2 or 3am. I didn't want the one late-night to make me exhausted for the rest of the week or take a risk of becoming run down, so I would sleep in. My early morning routine was changed for a good reason, an out-of-hours work commitment, and by being flexible I knew I would be able to happily recommence my 5am routine the next day.

Other times may not be so extreme, such as simply catching up with friends and not getting to bed before midnight (or later) after a few glasses of red wine.

Milo (left) Marcel (centre) and Bryce (right)
It's always ok to enjoy life!

You will begin to understand your own sleep requirements and may decide that your 5am routine be put on hold the following morning so you don't become run down.

There will be other times that you have to do this but as long as you rationally decide your waking time the night before with good reason, go ahead and be flexible. The last thing we want to happen is that you undertake this challenge at the expense of still being able to socialise responsibly, meet unusual work commitments, or simply enjoy life. That would only be setting you up for failure.

However, as you are in control of your own life and can usually decide the time you go to sleep, becoming a 5amer will need a purposeful change in lifestyle. The regular routine of staying up late watching *Letterman*, regularly staying out 'til late, or drinking too much will have to stop!

It's your choice.

"I am careful not to confuse excellence with perfection. Excellence, I can reach for; perfection is God's business."

–Michael J. Fox

Play #10: Be Kind to Yourself

We are aiming to build a long lasting enjoyable habit, not an impractical set of rules that will kick you when you are down! So be kind to your self.

Allowing yourself a break from early rising when you are unwell will:

1. Remove a reason to stop the habit permanently, thinking you have failed;
2. Allow you to recover faster and get back on track with your dreams;
3. Promote healthier living generally as the downtime from being sick becomes more apparent.

You are not a super hero and sometimes your body and mind may need the rest to recover from illness. This may be as simple as a bad cold or unfortunately worse, but sleep will allow you to recover faster and get back into your 5am routine.

Be honest with yourself so you don't start using the slightest sniffle or headache as an excuse to sleep in but if required, decide the day before that it is preferable to get more sleep, and revise your wake up plans before you go to bed. When you are ill it may also be good to go to bed even earlier so your routine is interrupted as little as possible, whilst giving your body as much rest as you can.

Be kind when you're sick and take a rest day.

Please remember, the purpose of your early rising routine is to set yourself up for success, not failure. You want to be strong, energised, and in good health to take on your magnificent obsession as best you can. This is not a habit that must be endured at the expense of your health and well-being. For most of us, we are not training for the Navy

SEALs or trying to set a new record for early rising, so allow your body extra recovery time during periods of ill health.

As I said, be kind to yourself when you are unwell.

Before we move on, please also understand that the overall 5am wake up call habit, with its promotion of exercise, good nutrition, and healthy lifestyle, will help reduce the number of sick days you experience.

Personally, I have never had a better appreciation that health and well-being far outweigh money, work, or any of the other usual measurements of success. Use your habit to make your body and mind as fit and strong as possible for the journey ahead.

"If you have health, you probably will be happy, and if you have health and happiness, you have all the wealth you need, even if it is not all you want."

–Elbert Hubbard

Play #11: The Alarm Clock

Your waking moments must be as pleasurable as possible to stimulate positive feelings about the golden minutes you are about to live!

Using an alarm clock is an essential tool for the 5amer that will help in three important ways:

1. Wake you up reliably at a pre-determined time and day;
2. Stimulate positive feelings and therefore the hormones that help make this experience desirable;
3. Make the habit easy to organise, manage, and maintain, no matter how busy you are, where you wake, and whom you wake up next to.

So, although every one has easy access to an alarm clock these days it is important to understand that each morning this is going to be the first trigger for waking up and making focussed and purposeful changes to your life.

The simple alarm clock is your essential tool that will help you make a million dollars, lose all the weight you desire, improve your health and fitness, write that best seller and create the life you have always dreamed of.

Don't underrate this; it is a very important tool indeed!

First of all, it is essential that your alarm clock is reliable so that it doesn't fail and become a reason (or excuse) for not waking up when you planned. For this to happen it must be easy to set up, allow scheduling for different days of the week as determined by your rules (e.g. week days only) and automatically repeat or re-set after it has been turned off each morning.

The modern day alarm clock, your million-dollar tool.

Secondly, it has to be as enjoyable as possible. Trust me, I know you may laugh at that notion, but it will become pleasurable (over time).

We all have different anger points so don't choose an alarm that is going to annoy you first thing in the morning. You want your alarm to become neurologically linked with pleasure not pain. Gone are the days of a noisy and confronting alarm rudely stopping your slumber with a loud buzz or bell; throwing those alarms against the wall or out the window was probably the best option. Now you can choose an alarm that suits your own taste so that you are kindly awakened with a sound that is going to gently remind you to get up so you can work on your dreams. I personally use my iPhone as it has good alarm settings, a pleasant alarm sound and is transportable. But you could use a clock radio, Bose System, Android phone, or almost any other digital device.

Never use the snooze button and when the alarm goes off you need to get out of bed straight away. Don't listen to the adolescent and don't change your plans. Think of your Magnificent Obsession and how fantastic it is that you are working toward its achievement, and get out of bed.

The exception to the snooze button rule is if you want to spend a few minutes before rising from bed for gratitude (as Darren Hardy does), to briefly review your day and set up your mind set as a 5amer. But make this brief (no more than one snooze) and then spring out to take the day head on.

Additionally, I also have a digital clock on the table next to the bed without the alarm set so I'm able to simply raise my head and see what time it is whenever I stir throughout the night. I now have an uncanny knack of looking at the alarm a few minutes before it goes off.

"The alarm in the morning? Well, I have an old tape of Carlo Maria Giulini conducting the Vienna Philharmonic Orchestra in a perfectly transcendent version in Shubert's seventh symphony. And I've rigged it up so that at exactly 7:30 every morning, it falls from the ceiling onto my face."

— Stephen Fry

Play #12: Preparation

Don't start the day disorganised, busy, or overwhelmed; be ready to take life head on, working toward achieving your goals. Prepare the night before.

By being well prepared the night before, you will:

1. Feel better about getting up in the morning, knowing you are set for action;
2. Enjoy smoother running mornings without stress or busy-ness.
3. Maximise the super-productivity of that golden hour or two.

Have your clothes all ready so you don't even have to think about it or so you're not looking for that lost sock or favourite shirt in the early hours of the morning.

If you need to take your lunch with you the next day, get it ready the night before so all you have to do is get it out of the fridge. I'll even fill up two water bottles at night so all I have to do the next morning is walk into the study and start hydrating with one while I dress, and throw the other into my gym bag on my way out.

Prepare the night before to maximise your morning super-productivity.

By the way, we don't want to get our wives, husbands, partners, or housemates off side every morning by banging around the bedroom or kitchen getting organised! We need them to support our habit (even if they don't want to actually do it themselves) so, be considerate and as quiet as you can while they **dream** about your success!

Most importantly, we need a strong reason for becoming a 5amer, so think about what you are going to do in the morning the night before. At the risk of over emphasising this point (mindset) you must be excited about what you will do when you wake up.......working on your million dollar idea, writing that book, losing weight, getting fit, or arriving at work early to initiate a promotion. When you go to sleep, you will feel content and calm, knowing how great the next morning is going to be and how you look forward to springing out of bed, wanting to get on with it.

"I've always considered myself to be just average talent and what I have is a ridiculous insane obsessiveness for practice and preparation."

– Will Smith

Play #13: Gain Strength from Your Partner

The last thing you want is to have a partner who works against your desire to improve your life.

Gaining strength from your partner or spouse will:

1. Add to your motivation, momentum, and focus so that you are more likely to succeed with your habit and the incredible dream you have;
2. Improve your relationship overall as you become more desirable;
3. Increase your own happiness, health and sense of success.

It is far too easy to drift away from your partner in life, especially when it comes to forging a new habit at the beginning of the day that changes who you are.

The first rule of a 5amer is don't push your new habit onto your partner.

The second rule of a 5amer is don't push your new habit onto your partner! (Yes, that was a reference to *Fight Club*, sorry.)

So if your partner doesn't want to wake up when you do, **<u>do not</u>** disturb them!

Look after your partner in life.

"But how can I do that when I'm using an alarm clock?"

Use a very soft one that has a soothing alarm (sounds a contradiction, but I'm sure you know what I mean). In fact, I have my iPhone set to silent and just wake up with the vibrating sound on the carpet (not bedside table). As your new routine develops into a habit you will be able to wake up with a very quiet and unintimidating alarm, on silent vibrate, or even before the alarm goes off.

It will also help if you include your partner in your enthusiasm and good fortune (once they wake up). We want our family to be pushing us towards success by being supportive and part of our cheer quad; so be considerate when you wake up and tell them about all the good things you are achieving. However, I have a strong warning! Don't jam your achievements down their throats by talking on and on about your success; show them tentatively with your results, they will pick up on it, and be impressed.

Understand that you are changing your own life and this may make them feel uneasy (change will usually do this), vulnerable, or even jealous. Fortunately, as they see the benefits to your life and your modesty, they are going to be more understanding, less critical, and may even give it a go!

"It is probably not love that makes the world go around, but rather those mutually supportive alliances through which partners recognize their dependence on each other for the achievement of shared and private goals."

–Fred Allen

Play #14: Love Your Weekends

The weekends are meant to recharge your batteries, not wipe you out so Monday morning is hell. So limit changing your habit on the weekends.

Now that you're a 5amer, if you take on your weekends with the same enthusiasm (even if you get to sleep in) you will:

1. Enjoy an hour or two of extra sleep each night without radically changing your sleep pattern;
2. Continue a fit and healthy lifestyle;
3. Enjoy family, friends, and life in general to its fullest!

Being a 5amer will change your life and without a doubt these changes will naturally include the weekends as well. If you like to go out on a Friday or Saturday night until the early hours of the morning and sleeping in all day, you may be in for a shock. Your habit of going to bed early and getting up early has changed who you are; being a 5amer is now part of your nature, identity, and purpose, and you love it.

For those not ready to accept this, who think that Friday night is still meant to be spent partying all night, I can guarantee that after 5 days of waking up at 5am your night life stamina will be totally shot, and around midnight you'll be ready for bed. Go with it, you can still have loads of fun but hopefully now you'll be more motivated and excited that you are living your dreams. The appeal of going out all-night and sleeping late will fade..........boring? I don't think so.

"I think it's more boring to have missed out on living your dream life! "

Look at Richard Branson, for example. He can still have fun and party but you don't see him falling out of the nightclubs at 3am!

It's up to you, who do you want to be?

However, we all need to enjoy life, socialise with our friends and family, and live life to the fullest. After all, you have done a great job with your new routine all week and are working very hard on your dreams, so you should be very proud of yourself. Let your hair down on the weekend and go out with your friends, take a trip, see a movie, and enjoy your rewards. Take a weekend off. But, listen to your body clock; it has changed! Remember who you are now, that has changed as well, so plan your nights out before you're influenced by your friends and alcohol. Decide when you are coming home and put procedures in place to make sure it happens; book a cab, let your friends know when you expect to go home, and go easy on the drinks.

Try to include exercise on your weekends as well. I have my alarm set for 5:40am on Saturdays (you see, a sleep in) so I can still go down to the surf club for a work out or pool for a swim with my surf lifesaving patrol. It's great! Oh, and on Sundays, I don't set any alarm at all, so I usually sleep in 'til 7:30 or 8:00am. You see, that weekend routine is not working against me.

Enjoy your weekends by living life big.

Remember why you have chosen the 5amer's life. Remember your dream. Remember who you want to be and take care so that you don't let the weekends work against that.

"I miss Saturday morning, rolling out of bed, not shaving, getting into my car with my girls, driving to the supermarket, squeezing the fruit, getting my car washed, taking walks."

–Barack Obama

Play #15: Enjoy Your Holidays

There's a time for waking up at 5 to take the world on and there's a time to chill out and enjoy time with friends and family.

Flexibility is the key to success, so including time out from waking at 5am as part of your strategy will:

1. Allow you to maintain a success mindset by removing any thought that you have failed to maintain your habit;
2. Let you enjoy your break without any guilt;
3. Make friends and family your biggest fan by showing them they matter, by taking time out to be with them.

As there are so many different types of holidays, it is important that you plan carefully how you are going to treat them as part of your 5amer life. Each holiday will need to be treated differently depending on where you are going, what you are doing, who you are going with, and how long you are going.

When you are planning your holiday remind yourself of why you have chosen your way of living and look at how your holiday is going to play a useful and strategic part of your plans.

If you're going away for a few days, or a week, you may just want to treat yourself to a break and enjoy the sleep in to recharge your battery and spend time with friends and family. Treat it like a weekend; after all, a week or so of a different routine will be fine.

Bryce and Fiona holidaying in Pisa, Italy.
(Sorry it just had to be done!)

If you are staying at home for a week or more, maybe continuing with your early morning routine is going to give you a chance to boost your Magnificent Obsession without all the other things you do in the day, such as work. How good are you going to feel by the end of a week and how much will you achieve?

You may be lucky enough to be going on an extended holiday over three months or more, travelling cross country or overseas with your family or a friend, backpacking or in an RV. In this case, you would be able to continue your 5am wake up call, utilising the early hours to continue working on your Magnificent Obsession if possible. You may be writing a book, losing weight, getting fit, or learning a new skill, all of which can continue as you travel. How good are you going to feel knowing that you are still achieving your dreams whilst enjoying the wonders of travel? Otherwise, utilise the early hours to plan your day, go for a walk and watch how the new culture starts the day, or make your short term Magnificent Obsession getting the most out of your holiday.

Whatever the situation, enjoy the break. Simply having a holiday without waking up early is going to recharge your batteries and allow you to start again when you get home with renewed vigour. You may prefer to continue with your 5am routine, knowing that the benefits it gives you will make your holiday all the more enjoyable by giving you a nice mix of achievement and relaxation — after all, you are working on your dream, not someone else's. Or, you may decide on a mix of both options by implementing a 5am wake up call only when it's practical, knowing you will be staying up later enjoying your holiday, but still not wanting to break the pattern too much.

Remember, it takes about a month to create a habit, so if you have a well established routine of rising early it would take about a month of sleeping-in for you to be out of the habit and more often than not, being a 5amer, you're not going to want to do that, so relax and enjoy.

"Stay committed to your decisions, but stay flexible in your approach."

–Tony Robbins

Play #16: Exercise Your Brain

Waking up early with purposeful thought day after day is no different than a daily workout at the gym; it's only your mind that is growing, not your muscles!

Your daily habit of waking up early with focussed thought and action towards a new rich life will promote neuroplasticity because:

1. Neurons that fire together, wire together, creating strong and fast pathways that changes thinking habits;
2. Thought with passion and emotion will release neurotransmitters such as dopamine that encourage you to repeat the experience and bring about neuroplasticity;
3. The competitive nature of the brains pathways old (bad) habits can be overrun by new (beneficial) habits.

As mentioned earlier in this book, it is important to exercise your brain with care as it has the ability to change directly as a result of those thoughts and actions through the process of neuroplasticity.

When you get up at 5am, utilise the way you think with care as you are literally rewiring your brain. Think about how good it is that you are now actively working on your dream (your magnificent obsession). Be clear in your thinking so you are making the neurons in your brain become familiar with your definite purpose and strong, fast pathways will be energised, and habits developed.

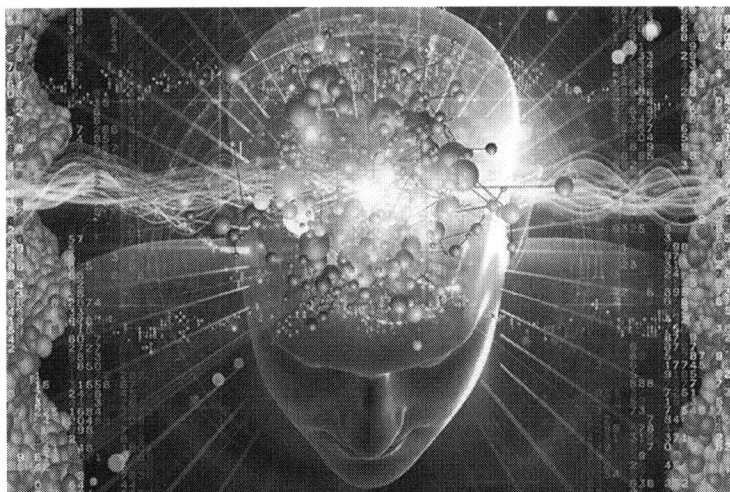

The power of the mind will create your New Rich Life.

When this is done again and again each morning over weeks, months, and even better years, you will have developed a way of thinking that is now hard wired. Not only will being the 5amer become easier and part of who you are, but you will also be driven to working hard towards your Magnificent Obsession until it is achieved.

Purposely take full control those waking thoughts as well as how you think and feel during the first one or two hours. Exercise your brain, build a strong mindset, and carry that throughout your day.

In addition to this, when I wake up I write out a daily Magnificent Obsession Statement. The activity of writing out what I'm working towards, when I want to achieve that specific success, and what I'm prepared to do by way of action forges strong and fast neurological pathways. Like I said, it becomes a habit, or put simply; the way I think. That is then carried over into the rest of the day, in fact, the rest of my life; it determines who I am and who I am known to be!

There is no better time in the day than the morning to exercise the power of neuroplasticity as the brain is fresh, after computing yesterday's data overnight, and you are free of distractions, busy-ness and the demands from others (and our commitments).

Put this into practice and you will be jumping out of bed ready to take life head on, completely out of habit!

"I will not let anyone walk through my mind with their dirty feet."

– Mahatma Gandhi

Play #17: Persistence, Persistence, Persistence

Rarely does success come knocking at the door, it takes persistence until it is tracked down and pushed into submission.

Understanding the power of persistence:

1. Removes the frustration that usually results when dreams aren't realised as initially desired so that you can continue the journey;
2. Allows you to appreciate the journey as much as the achievement of success;
3. Makes success all the more gratifying – hard won gains will always taste better than gifts from luck.

Don't let failure stop you from starting again. The life of the 5amer is very forgiving as each new morning brings a new start. If you fail to rise in your waking minutes don't let that prevent you from utilising this powerful strategy for developing a habit to help achieve your dream. Simply set the alarm for the very next morning and use the principles outlined in this book to start again.

If you fail again, reassess the reason for the shortcoming and try again.

If you fail again, reassess the reason for the shortcoming and try again.

And then, if you still fail, reassess the reason for the shortcoming and try again!

Persistence will always result in success as long as you learn from your failures, change your strategy, and stay the course.

I love the story Tony Robins often recalls regarding persistence and a client of his who was trying to make a change in his life. It goes something like this.

Client – "I have tried everything, but none of it works! It's all useless and I cannot see the point for going on!"
Tony – "So, you've tried everything?"
Client – "Yes, everything!"
Tony – "So let me just get this clear, you've tried… ten thousand different ways?"
Client – "Well, not ten thousand ways…but lots!"
Tony – "So, two hundred ways then?"
Client – "Well, no! But more than I can remember anyway!"
Tony – "Okay…so a hundred?"
Client –"No, not one hundred!"

Tony –"So how many ways have you actually tried?"

Client –"Well, at least a dozen!"

Tony –"Name them! Go on, name the twelve ways you have tried to change this!"

Client –"Okay, so maybe it's only three or four! But I simply give up...nothing works!!"

Tony –"Now let's get this clear, you have come here because it hasn't worked after trying three maybe four different ways to fix this...so you can live the life you really want...your dream life!"

Client – silence...more silence...

Tony –"Well?"

Client –"I suppose I could give it another go."

If it takes 50 clocks to wake up, find 50 clocks!

So, when you think you have tried it all, remind yourself of the ten thousand experiments it took Thomas Edison to invent the light bulb; or the three or so hundred mornings it took John Grisham to write the first draft of *A Time to Kill,* page by page; or the millions of balls Tiger Woods hit before he improved that half a per cent to make it to the top.

Keep trying every morning until you work out what works for you and you will make early rising a habit.

Then apply that habit to whatever you chose to do with those golden minutes at the crack of dawn, and you will succeed!

"I do not think that there is any other quality so essential to success of any kind as the quality of perseverance. It overcomes almost everything, even nature."

– John D. Rockefeller

Play #18: Good Health and Fitness

We all need to be athletes. That is, if you want to live your dreams by achieving success with your Magnificent Obsession anyway.

Treating your personal health and fitness as a "must" rather than a "should" will:

1. Give you the energy and peak state to persist at achieving your dream life;
2. Allow you to enjoy both the journey and the success when it finally comes;
3. Make waking up early the highlight of your day, knowing what wonders lie ahead.

To wake up each morning with energy and drive, you must have good health and fitness. You must eat well, rest well, exercise, stay on top of your health, and treat yourself like an athlete. As I have said many times, this is not about getting less sleep, this is not about burning yourself out, and this is not about going through the tough times, battling towards success.

This is about taking life head on, with strength and power.

Thousands of books have been written about health and fitness covering specifics such as loosing weight, exercise, diet and nutrition and so on; which indicates the importance of this play.

While living a full life as a 5amer you should be concerned with all of it (health and fitness); and it must become a priority in your day.

Make health and fitness your number one priority.

As I have experimented with making a 5am wake up call my habit to live by for more than 10 years now I have utilised my early hours for many different challenges and goals. I initially started walking along the beach at about 5:20am (after stretching and writing my daily magnificent obsession statement). Even though I had never been a runner, after months of walking I had a massive desire to start jogging. I absolutely fell in love with it and so jogging has become a strong foundation for my early morning fitness habit. Things change, but even during the years I arrived at work at 5:30am (instead of heading to the beach) to find the time to plan, strategize, eventually prepare and successfully sell the business, I made sure that exercise was scheduled into my day. It was my priority and I was determined to stick to it!

I then spent a few years writing my book during the hours of 5:15am to 7:30am (page by page, just like John Grisham) but again, I made sure exercise was included in my routine.

And today as I write this Playbook, I am back to an early morning exercise routine: 6:00am at the surf club gym followed by a swim in the surf (and a coffee in the club). I then return for a big (healthy) breakfast, take my daughter to school, and start writing.

Throughout these changing times, I have managed to include exercise (in varying degrees) as part of the mix...as I said, it's my priority.

So don't let the drive for success make your own health and fitness suffer. As far as I'm concerned, and as a 5amer, that is not success at all.

"There comes a certain point in life when you have to stop blaming other people for how you feel or the misfortunes in your life. You can't go through life obsessing about what might have been."

– Hugh Jackman

Play #19: Strong New Rich Life Foundations

Being a 5amer means you now have time to work on all the foundations to a New Rich Life!

As outlined in previous Plays, having a dream to focus on is essential for waking up at 5am. Symbiotically, finding your Magnificent Obsession and working on it with focus, persistence and discipline are the benefits of your habit.

Your Magnificent Obsession will be rocketed to greater heights by the following New Rich Life Foundations:

1. Health and Fitness – Now you have time to stay fit and be as healthy as you can, which will make meeting the challenge easier;
2. Friends and Family – Get on top of the day so you can spend time with your friends and family and they will become your biggest fans, supporting your habit and pushing you towards success;
3. Happiness – Much unhappiness comes from not doing what you desire. Working towards your magnificent obsession increases happiness, which, in turn motivates you to keep going;
4. Wealth – The desire to become *The 5am Millionaire* (the title of my upcoming book) will motivate your

habit, and be a result of all the energy you have focused towards those goals.

5. Work – Do you have a dream job? If not, now you have the time before work to requalify, research, and re-apply!

As we have just re-affirmed, this is not a habit to tip you over the edge in an unbalanced life. This is a habit that requires you be in top form in all the foundations of your new rich life.

You must be fit and healthy so you can maintain the energy and be at your peak.

You need to be happy and motivated so you can spring out of bed each morning knowing you are going to have a great day.

You need a clear understanding that you are on the way to creating wealth and riches but more importantly, what that wealth and riches actually means to you.

The 5am Millionaire......
Your New
Rich Life!

Magnificent Obsession

Health & Fitness | Happiness | Friends & Family | Money $$$$$$ | Work

The 5amer's New Rich Life Strategy

You're going to have more time to be with your good friends and family, doing the things you love doing, so wake up knowing that is all ahead of you.

Organise your work so it supports your habit, and if you need to go to work early, and it's not part of your dream, finish early so you can plan, work towards and live your dream with purpose, later in the day. All the strategies outlined in this book will be applicable for most work situations, but it may take a high level of creativity, flexibility, and focus.

So take support from your rich life foundations so they can make this habit achievable and enjoyable.

"If you're interested in 'balancing' work and pleasure, stop trying to balance them. Instead, make your work more pleasurable."

– Donald Trump

Play #20: The End Play

Often when we search for the smaller answers in life, bigger insights become abundant and life as we knew it is never the same.

Congratulations! You have just about completed the 5am Playbook to make waking up at 5am a long lasting and enjoyable habit!

The final step may appear to be some what contradictory, but I'll say it anyway.

It's all right if you don't wake up at 5:00am!

What! Being a 5amer is *not* all about waking up at 5am?

Well, yes it is all about waking up at 5am, but it's also much more than that.

Being a 5amer is about finding the time each day with discipline and persistence to focus on your burning desire, your magnificent obsession. And, to successfully achieve your magnificent obsession, you must be rocketed up by your health and fitness, friends and family, happiness, wealth, and work – the foundations of your new rich life.

Accordingly, all I ask is that you wake up earlier than normal to find this time. 5:00am has worked best for me but I'm good with 5:30am, or even 6:00am, as you will still be able to realise the power of this habit.

But please be careful and honest with yourself, you have the ability to wake up at 5:00am and I highly recommend you give it a go (see Play #3 – Set the Rules).

The aim is to find the time in a busy life that is dedicated to YOU!

For those who are night owls, I am not trying to convert you! Well, maybe a little bit, but that's okay. If being a night owl is definitely how you want to live, please go ahead, but please save some time at the end of the day to work with focus on your dreams. This is harder than doing it in the morning as you will have commitments that easily disrupt the best-laid intentions and you (and your brain) will be tired from processing the day's data. Again, be honest with yourself and open to the idea of giving early rising a try, even if it's just to achieve a short-term challenge or goal as a test.

As you can see, this book has morphed into much more than just being a guide to successfully wake up at 5am into the start of living a New Rich Life, as a 5amer.

What I'm suggesting is that by a simple change to your physical day, by rising to meet the day earlier, you have made a physical change to your life that will lead to many secondary corrections, including to one's self. With an early rising habit, you will find your own path in a productive and purposeful life.

Have you ever got to a certain place in life and said, "That's it, no more, that's enough!" Sometimes, as if by total accident, you end up in a place that you never dreamed of or planned to be. Well, now is the time in your life to take action! You can reset your life but that needs a significant jolt.

A 5am Wake Up Call (an early rising habit) can be that significant jolt to change your life. When you make a waking at 5am your daily habit you will have physically changed who you are. You will be someone who has taken control of your life, chosen to wake up and get on with the task of living life to the fullest, and who is working hard towards achieving your dreams. Those around you will see the change and have respect because you are proving that by being passionate about your life and working hard towards your dreams you have already found success. Whatever you choose to focus your 5am mornings on will develop, grow, and take momentum as you head towards its achievement.

Start a 5amer's life now and experience life to the fullest.

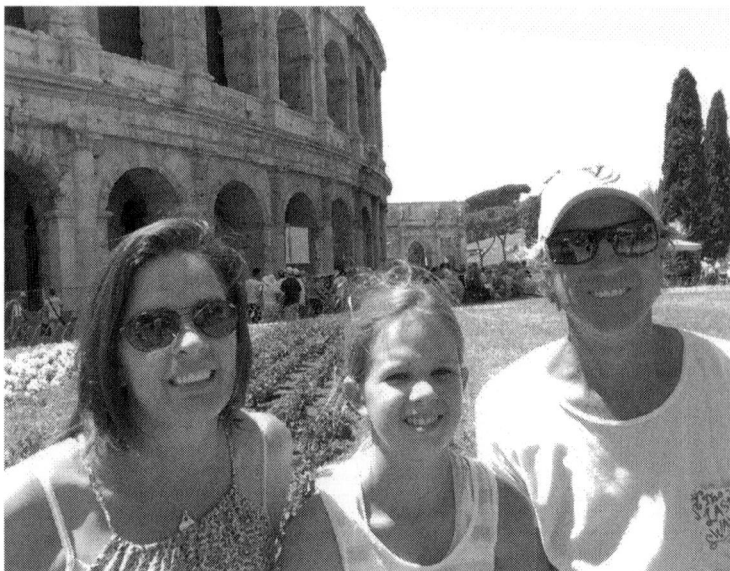

Bryce enjoying a holiday in Rome with wife Fiona
and daughter Brooke.

"Once you have mastered time, you will understand how true it is that most people overestimate what they can accomplish in a year – and underestimate what they can achieve in a decade."– Tony Robbins

Live with passion…

Bryce Chapman

Bryce Chapman
5amer

5am Wake Up Call
P.O. Box 900
Narrabeen, NSW, 2101
Australia

adventure@5amwakeupcall.com
www.5amwakeupcall.com

Printed in Great Britain
by Amazon